Belonging Abroad

A Guide to Living, Thriving, and
Appreciating New Cultures

Bruce Knotts

Belonging Abroad:
A Guide to Living, Thriving, and
Appreciating New Cultures
By Bruce Knotts

For information, contact
BDI Publishers, Atlanta, Georgia
bdipublishers@gmail.com

Cover Design and Layout: Tudor Maier
BDI Publishers

Atlanta, Georgia

ISBN: 978-1-946637-38-3

"Read this book and pack your bags! With wonderful storytelling, Bruce Knotts shares what he's learned from a lifetime of traveling, living, and working abroad, and how *you* can get the most out of every place you visit. Unlike the usual travel guide, he shows you how to stay grounded in your true self, even while you adapt to the new worlds you're discovering, because that's the magic of travel. And the first thing magic changes is you."

—Phyllis Curott, attorney, & author of the international best-seller *Book of Shadows, A Modern Woman's Journey into the Magic of the Goddesss*

"Bruce's concise book provides a wealth of practical advice, backed up by his real-life experiences from all over the world. This quickly provides Invaluable tips for anyone planning to explore a new and different country."

—David Overton President and CEO of NGO Committee on Disarmament, Peace, and Security

"Belonging Abroad is a journey into the world of travel which one can experience by taking the advice of the author. It gets us to think about the awesome adventures that await us in foreign lands. It took me back to my own memories of exciting trips I have taken around the world and the wonderful people I have met. For travelers who want to go back down memory lane or think of the next adventure that awaits, this book will help us appreciate the beauty of the world we live in."

—Sharan Kaur Singh Midwest Deputy Director for the Anti-Defamation League

"The perfect little big book to read along with travel guides for having delightful and meaningful encounters with people from other places, cultures and religions. Transforms strangers to friends, from separation to belonging, and through stories inspires us to be humble, curious, respectful and open to new adventures even if we don't travel."

—Ann Smith Co-Founder and Facilitator of the Green Tent Circle

"This concise monograph is a page turner from the first paragraph to the last. It is indispensable reading for anyone travelling abroad, but the author's fascinating experiences of the world, told unpretentiously but with a master story-teller's flair, make it an absorbing read for most anyone. The overarching theme of the book is opening yourself to, and getting immersed in, what is new and different. The key is learning from and forming authentic relationships with local residents.

Folks from the United States—my country—tend to rely upon tried-and-true tourist resources and routines. While safe, they are also limiting. Author Bruce Knotts provides practical guidelines for ensuring your health and safety abroad, freeing you to venture off the beaten path of the tourist industry and connect meaningfully with the people, cultures, religions, food, sports, and customs of other countries. His book delivers every bit of what the title promises and more."

—Brian D'Agostino, Ph.D., author,
The Middle Class Fights Back

"In Belonging Abroad, Bruce Knotts offers a wise, deeply personal, and refreshingly honest guide to thriving across cultures. Drawing from decades of global experience—from Peace Corps postings to encounters with extraordinary individuals—he shows that the true passport to connection isn't privilege, but humility, curiosity, and the courage to step into the unfamiliar. This book is a gift for anyone seeking not just to travel, but to belong."

—Harpreet Singh, Harvard University

Contents

Introduction

At seventeen, Tyrone and I worked together, and after work, we went the Santa Monica beach and sat on the beach watching the waves. Suddenly, Tyrone kissed me. At first, I wanted to push him away, but I realized how much I loved his kiss, and I embraced him instead.

I told my mother that I was in love with Tyrone and asked her not to tell my father. She told him right away and both my parents were panicked by their gay son. To get me away from Tyrone, they sent me to Pepperdine University's program in Heidelberg, Germany. I missed Tyrone very much, but I also loved being in Heidelberg. Those years in Germany also included trips to Italy, and other neighboring countries. That cemented my love for living, studying and working in different countries. I never met Tyrone again, but I was hooked on living and working all around the world.

After Germany, I went on a two-year Peace Corps assignment in Ethiopia, which turned into three years. Living in Ethiopia wasn't easy.

My assigned town had no electricity or running water. But something happened along the way—I learned to adjust. And I found that I liked it. That early adjustment turned out to be one of the most valuable experiences of my life. Later, when I applied to the Foreign Service, those years living abroad gave me an edge. And not just on paper. Most people assigned overseas panic when they realize how different life can be outside of America. That panic can be expensive—not just for the individual, but for the organization that sent them. If a company pays to relocate you, gives you a house, maybe even a car, and you leave after a month or two, they've lost a lot. What they want—what any organization wants—is someone who can adapt. If you've already done it once—or twice—that says a lot about who you are.

Later on, I worked for Raytheon in Saudi Arabia, at the Air Defense School. My background in Heidelberg and the Peace Corps helped me land the job. They looked at my past and said, "If he could handle all that, we'll send him to Saudi Arabia." It wasn't exactly a vacation spot—but I didn't panic. I did my job, finished my assignment, and moved on.

Eventually, I worked under a World Bank contract in Somalia. That was a different kind of challenge. It wasn't a U.S. government post or a Peace Corps mission—it was the World Bank that sent me to Mogadishu. It was difficult. But again, I didn't panic. In fact, it turned out to be one of the most meaningful experiences I had. I even ordered a car and had it shipped. The port was known for corruption, and everyone expected I'd have to pay a bribe. But I stood my ground. I showed up with my paperwork, said, "My car is here. It's on the boat. I want to take possession of it. Here are my credentials." And eventually, I got it—without paying anyone off. That might seem like a small thing, but in that environment, it wasn't.

So yes, I've had a long history with international travel and overseas assignments. But this book isn't about me. It's about you. It's about how *you* can have more rewarding, insightful, and even joyful experiences abroad—whether it's your first trip or your fiftieth.

Maybe you're preparing for a semester overseas. Maybe you're taking on an international assignment for work. Or maybe you're just curious about what it's like to live in a place where the language, culture, and daily rhythm are completely different. Wherever you're headed, there's one thing I hope you'll take with you: the understanding that things will be different—and that difference is not something to fear.

When I moved from Silver Spring, Maryland to New York City, I was nervous. I thought *it would be dangerous and wildly expensive.*

While it is expensive, it wasn't nearly as crime-ridden as I had feared. Still, it took time to adjust. But I did. Now I've been here for more than twenty years. And I can tell you this: no matter where you go—whether to a different city in the U.S. or to another country—you'll need to figure things out. You'll need to learn. You'll need to adapt.

In a foreign country, the learning curve is steeper. You'll face differences in food, language, religion, and customs. Ethiopian food, for example, includes a bread called injera. The first time I tried it, I thought, *What on earth is this?* It has a sour taste and a sponge-like texture. But after a while, I came to love it. I even seek out Ethiopian restaurants here in New York now.

One of the biggest mistakes people make when traveling is assuming that if something looks or feels unfamiliar, it must be wrong. That's not true. It's just different. And different can be wonderful.

That's the mindset I want to encourage in this book: effort, curiosity, and humility. Because when you travel with those things, people notice. And they usually respond with warmth, generosity, and a willingness to share.

Imagine you're in Kathmandu. It's high in the mountains, the air is crisp, and nothing looks familiar. You don't speak the language. You don't recognize the food. It can feel overwhelming at first. But then—slowly—you find your rhythm. You meet people. You learn a few words. You get your bearings. And then something beautiful happens: the unfamiliar becomes familiar.

The real joy of travel doesn't come from snapping a photo or checking a destination off your list. It comes from connecting—with people, with culture, with history. It comes from letting go of control and stepping into something new.

Throughout this book, I'll share lessons I've learned from years of living, working, and traveling overseas. I'll tell you what worked, what didn't, and how to get the most out of every place you visit. And I'll show you how to stay grounded in who you are—even while adapting to everything around you.

Because that's the magic of travel: it stretches you. It challenges you. And if you let it, it changes you for the better.

So let's begin.

Chapter 1

How to Meet Key Individuals in a New Country

My mother sent me twenty dollars to give to Mother Teresa. I thought *it was a paltry amount*, so I added another twenty of my own, for a total of forty dollars. I put it in an envelope with a nice note. At the time, I was working at the Consulate General in Calcutta, where we had drivers. I asked one of them to deliver it to the Mother House for me.

When I got back to my apartment that evening, I heard the phone ringing. I started fiddling with the lock, trying to get the door open so I wouldn't miss the call. I made it just in time. I picked up the phone—and it was Mother Teresa herself, not someone calling on her behalf. She said, "That was a really nice note you sent me. Can I meet you?"

I thought, *Oh my God, can she meet me*? She's asking! I said, "Yes, of course." She said, "Can you come to the Mother House at 10 o'clock tomorrow?"

The next day, I went to the Mother House. I sat with her for over an hour, and she held my hand the whole time. I thought, *This living saint is holding my hand. I'm sitting here with a real saint. She really was saintly—there was something quite wonderful about her.* She believed she had received a divine message to help the poor people of Calcutta, and she truly seemed connected to the divine. While she sat holding my hand, I felt connected too.

The Sisters of Charity at the Mother House wanted to wash her clothes and sweep her floors, but she wouldn't let anyone do anything for her. She washed her own clothes. She swept her own floors. Even though all the sisters living there wanted to take care of her, she insisted on doing everything herself.

I think it frustrated them, especially since she was already in her eighties. She told me she wanted to send her Sisters of Charity to China. I thought, *Girlfriend, you're in your eighties. You've already done so much—and now you want to conquer China too?* I didn't say that out loud, but it definitely crossed my mind. When I asked if she was serious, she said, "Yes, I want to." I don't know whether she ever managed to send them or not.

Show Interest

When you're visiting or living in a different country, you'll meet people who are very different from you—and you'll be different to them too. Often, they'll be just as curious about you as you are about them. People will come up to you, ask where you're from, why you're there, what you're doing. Start talking, and you'll start building relationships. Ask them the same questions back, and you might really hit it off.

Find a Way to Help Others So You Can Build Meaningful Relationships

Mother Teresa also wanted to send her Sisters of Charity to the United States to care for dying AIDS patients that the U.S. government wasn't helping. It cost $100 to get a United States visa, and she explained they didn't want to use donated money just to pay government fees. She asked if we could waive the charges.

I told her I'd have to check with the consulate and see what I could do. I went to Catherine Burke, the visa officer, and explained the situation. Catherine's first reaction was, "Ah, let Elizabeth Taylor take care of the dying AIDS patients," since Elizabeth Taylor was famously campaigning for AIDS causes at the time.

A few days later, my secretary walked into my office. I was busy and cantankerous as usual. She said, "Bruce, you have a visitor downstairs."

I said, "Who the hell is it now?"

She said, "It's Mother Teresa."

I said, "Oh my God."

I ran downstairs, brought her up to my office, and sat her on my couch. Then I called Catherine Burke and said, "Hi Catherine, how are you? Remember what you said about Mother Teresa's visas? Well, she's in my office. Maybe you can come tell her yourself."

Catherine came upstairs and sat down next to Mother Teresa. Within minutes, Mother Teresa had her completely charmed. Catherine didn't mention Elizabeth Taylor again. She just said, "Okay, all right, we'll work this out. We'll see if we can get free visas for you."

It all came together quickly after that. We spoke with Ron Lorton, the Consul General at the time, and he agreed it was the right thing to do. Between the Consul General, the visa officer, and the rest of us, we made it happen. We started issuing visas to Mother Teresa's Sisters of Charity, allowing them to travel to the United States without paying the one hundred dollar fee.

Meanwhile, Delta Airlines had just started flying directly to Calcutta. I told the head of Delta my Mother Teresa story, and he said, "Well, tell Mother Teresa she's got a free seat on Delta anytime she wants."

Helping People

That's what I did with Mother Teresa, even though she was famous. It's what I try to do with everyone: say, "Oh, okay, you're working in a hospital? I'd love to visit and see what you're doing. Tell me what you need, what you're dealing with—maybe I can help or make some recommendations." Whatever it is, when you start helping people with what they care about, you build a real connection.

I also asked Mother Teresa what I could do for her personally. She said, "You could volunteer in my Home for the Dying."

My first thought was, *Oh my God. That's not what I want to do.* But because she asked, I did it.

Her Home for the Dying was a hospice for people pulled off the streets of Calcutta—people who were dying without care. Sometimes, after being fed and looked after, they survived. Sometimes they didn't. But at least they died receiving kindness and dignity.

At first, I found it creepy going there. I didn't want to be in that place. They had cement beds with risers, and many people were lying on them, straight from the streets. That's how Mother Teresa's mission began—by caring for people dying in the gutters of Calcutta. Most of the people in the Home for the Dying did pass away, but some survived, healed, and eventually left.

Just like I did with Mother Teresa, when you find out what people are doing with their lives, say, "I think what you're doing is amazing. How can I help or get involved?" It's a way to build rapport immediately. Most people care deeply about something or are helping in some way. If there's a place for you to contribute, they'll let you know—and they'll be glad you offered.

More Strategies to Win People Over

Ask for Help

When you're new somewhere, don't be afraid to ask questions. Say, "I'm brand new here. I don't know how to get to this place," or "I'm not sure how to handle this situation. Can you help me?"

People love to help when you give them the chance. Asking for help—and giving it—is one of the fastest ways to build rapport.

Eat

Another simple but powerful thing: food.

Sometimes people will invite you to their home for dinner. It doesn't matter how much they have or where they live—food brings everyone together. Even if they take you to a small restaurant, food will almost always be part of building relationships.

Sometimes the food might seem strange to Americans. But if you eat it—and show you enjoy it—you'll win people over. If you refuse, you might lose an opportunity to connect.

Don't Be Afraid to Speak Out

For a time, I served as the Executive Director of the Department of Public Information Council at the United Nations, representing 2,000 nonprofits. Many people thought I was a high-ranking United Nations official, but really, I was representing non-governmental organizations.

Somehow, the World League for Freedom and Democracy heard about me and invited me to speak at their annual conference in 2017.

I traveled there with my husband, introduced him to the audience, and immediately started talking about something that mattered deeply to me: same-sex marriage. I even met with President Ma, the sitting president of the country, to speak about it.

At the World League, there were legislators from around the world—including a good friend of mine, Senator Diarmuid Wilson from Ireland. He invited my husband and me to visit Ireland. We toured the Irish Senate, and later he took us out to dinner at a nearby restaurant. We meet up every year now at the World League. Once, he even took me to an Irish pub in Taipei. I didn't even know they had an Irish pub, but he knew exactly where it was. I built a lot of strong relationships—not just with Taiwanese people, but with visitors from all over the world.

Eventually, I became instrumental in helping Taiwan pass same-sex marriage.

At one point, the Presbyterian Church in Taiwan pushed for a referendum against it, and most voters opposed same-sex marriage. Afterward, I gave a speech that became front-page news across the country. I said, "You cannot vote against people's human rights. The majority will always vote against the minority."

That quote became part of the national debate. When the legislature discussed the issue, one side pointed to the referendum, and the other side pointed to my words. And they won the day: the legislature passed same-sex marriage, making Taiwan the first country in Asia to do so.

To sum up: it doesn't take much to meet key individuals when you're traveling—a small contribution and a nice note can go a long way. In my case, that was all it took to build a relationship with Mother Teresa and help her Sisters of Charity.

And if you believe in a cause, don't be afraid to speak your mind. You might just change history.

Chapter 2

Be Humble and Ask Questions

I remember visiting La Scala, the best opera house in the world, in Milan. I didn't have much money, so I sat in the nosebleed section at the top. An American couple was sitting in front of me as we listened to a beautiful soprano. At one point, they said, "Oh, she's excellent. She could probably make it to the Met."

I just sat there thinking, *We're at La Scala, and they're talking about The Met?* It felt like they were suggesting that The Met was better. That kind of ignorance and lack of humility can make it tough to enjoy your experiences outside of the United States. When you're traveling, two of the most important things you can do are to be humble and ask questions. That's why, in this chapter, you'll learn how humility and asking questions can make traveling overseas a much richer experience.

Don't Ask for "American" Things - You're Not in America

Another time, I was in a restaurant next to the Stazione Termini in Rome. I was ordering my food when I heard an American woman insist, "I want some sugar. It has to be American sugar. Is this American sugar? I must have American sugar."

I thought, *Really? Sugar is sugar anywhere in the world.*

That kind of attitude makes me cringe, especially when I see it coming from Americans abroad. When you approach situations with that kind of arrogance, you miss out on the very experience you traveled to have.

And it's not just Americans—British, French, and pretty much any group can sometimes act in an arrogant manner while abroad. But if you go with humility, you'll enjoy yourself—and the place—so much more.

How Humility and Asking Questions Can Help You Have a Positive Experience

When you're in another country, don't assume things are done the same way they are back home.

Americans often do business through paperwork, emails, or sending things along quickly. But in many countries, you can't move forward without building personal relationships. That's something I loved about the book *Three Cups of Tea* by David Oliver Relin and Greg Mortenson—it captures that idea perfectly. In a lot of cultures, business doesn't start until you've sat down, had a cup of tea, gotten to know each other—and sometimes done it again and again.

Before I traveled to Kenya, we needed all sorts of special access at the Calcutta Airport—access to the VIP lounge, special luggage handling, and other arrangements for a Congressional visit. To get all that set up, I made the rounds at the airport, having tea with everyone with whom I needed to work.

By the time I got to the last person, a man named Treasurywala, I was practically swimming in tea.

I said, "Do I really have to have another cup? I've had so much tea my eyeballs are about ready to float." He smiled and said, "Oh yes, you do."

So I had another cup of tea. And we sat, and we talked. It was important to him—and in his culture, it meant something. Later, if I had just called and said, "We have a Congressional visit coming and need special services," without those conversations, it would have been *Click*—no help. But because I had those cups of tea, I wasn't just a name on the phone. I was a person they knew.

And that's how it works in many parts of the world: you're not just a request; you're a relationship.

The same thing happened when I was in Cluj, Romania. I was admiring these magnificent old buildings, and I asked a local person about them. She lit up when I showed interest. She explained that they used to be government buildings, homes for princes and royalty. Today, they're hotels and offices, but the history remains in every stone.

She said she was grateful I asked. Those buildings meant a lot to her, and she was proud to share their story. And because I asked, I got a deeper appreciation not just for the buildings, but for Romania itself.

She told me about Romania's strong Hungarian influence and how much of their royal history came from Hungary. It wasn't something I knew before—and I wouldn't have learned it if I hadn't asked.

I try to do that everywhere I go. I'll see something beautiful or intriguing and simply ask about it. People are usually eager to tell you their stories— whether it's about a building, a piece of food, or their own life.

And it turns a beautiful building into something even richer. It turns a nice meal into a memory. It turns a place into a story you'll carry with you.

Having the Right Mindset

Don't be afraid to ask questions. If you see something beautiful or interesting, ask someone about it. People are usually excited to share their stories and their culture.

Even a simple question like, "Tell me your story," can open the door to an amazing conversation.

And remember: things will be different. Places, food—even sugar—won't be what you're used to. But that's the point. You didn't travel halfway around the world to have everything be just like home.

Be ready to eat the local food. Be ready to take the sugar you're given. Be ready for hotel rooms that don't look like the ones in America. Toilets, sinks, and showers might be different too. But don't get indignant. They won't redesign their country just because you're uncomfortable.

If you don't know how to use something or need help, ask. People are usually happy to explain. But saying things like, "Why isn't it like America?" just makes you look foolish. Because you're not in America—you're somewhere new. And you're there to learn and experience something different.

When you travel, leave your home country in the rearview mirror. Focus on where you are.

Don't compare—experience.

That's the real reason you're traveling: to see something new, to broaden your world, and to appreciate how rich and varied life is across the globe.

Questions You Can Ask

- Tell me a little bit about yourself.
- Tell me about this city.
- What should I see when I'm here?
- What's interesting to see in (fill in name of city)?
- Where is the food from?
- What ingredients are in the food?
- Is this what people like to eat here?
- Is this a celebratory food?

If you stay open, ask questions, and bring some humility, you'll walk away with far richer, more memorable experiences than you ever could by sticking to what you already know.

Chapter 3

Other Ways to Have Fun

Having fun can change your entire perspective.

My husband once visited Uganda and went on a photo safari. Later, after he returned, we visited the San Diego Zoo. It's one of America's great zoos—you can see giraffes, lions, and elephants there, but they're all in cages.

After a while, my husband said, "I have to leave." I asked, "Why?" He said, "I can't take this anymore. I just saw all these animals free and moving how they wanted to in the wild. I can't watch them locked up in cages."

So, we left the zoo and went to a nice restaurant instead.

That experience changed his mindset—and it's a good example of how having fun in different ways can shift the way you see the world. In this chapter, I'll share a few other experiences like that.

Be Open to New Experiences

When I worked at the U.S. Embassy, I was assigned as the contact person for a delegation from Senator Hillary Clinton's office. We took them to a concert featuring Guinean drummers and dancers.

The Senate staff couldn't get over it. The music was incredible, and they were completely enamored with the dancers, who were beautiful and full of energy.

This wasn't some formal stadium performance. We were outside, among the trees. The drummers brought their drums, and the music filled the air. African drumming—especially in West Africa— is spectacular. The rhythm and dexterity are like nothing you'll see at concerts in the United States. It wasn't just entertainment; it was education. It showed what other cultures consider entertainment and how different—and beautiful—that can be.

As a Californian, I've visited many wineries. But in Stellenbosch, just outside Cape Town, South Africa, the wineries are something else. Not only do they offer amazing wine, but many of them also have Michelin-star restaurants right on-site. You can sit down for lunch, have a fabulous meal, and enjoy spectacular wine— all surrounded by beautiful Dutch colonial architecture, a legacy of South Africa's Dutch history.

I loved my time there. After Cape Town, I drove to Durban, stopped to hike in the forests, and saw breathtaking views of the Atlantic Ocean crashing against the rocks. You can't imagine the experiences you'll have if you stay open to broadening your horizons.

Tips for Having Fun and Finding Experiences that Stay with You for a Long Time

Explore and Look for Exciting Things you Haven't Seen Before

Sometimes, you have to go beyond the tourist books. Ask people what you should see—it's often music, dance, or something cultural, because people are proud of their heritage. Africans, in particular, take great pride in music, dancing, and singing.

Think About What You Really Enjoy

Whenever you go, there are always mountains, valleys, waterfalls, oceans, but there's also performance, music, food, and culture to experience.

And sometimes, getting involved in local religious traditions can be fascinating.

Many Africans still practice indigenous beliefs, and it's interesting to see how marriage ceremonies, rituals, and traditions differ from what you might be used to.

Even Christianity and Islam, which are widespread across Africa, feel different. In Africa, the music in a Christian church service has an unmistakable African beat. It's a unique experience compared to what you'd hear in a church in the United States.

Be Mindful of Signs Posted in the Places You Visit

When we visited Lake Manyara National Park in Tanzania, the first thing I noticed was a funny sign:

"Take No Liberties with the Animals."

I thought, *What does that even mean? I wasn't planning to!*

Then, a little while later, we were in a van and saw a male elephant. He started charging at us—with a full erection.

We started moving very quickly because he was headed straight toward us at full speed. I'm still not sure what he thought we were, but he wanted to take some liberties with us. Needless to say, we got out of there fast.

Think About How You Want to Get Where You're Going

There are so many different ways to travel. For example, in Kenya, it's fun to take the train from Nairobi to Mombasa. Most tourists don't think about it, but it's a fantastic way to see the countryside. The British built the railway during colonial times, and although the cars and engines have been updated, the route is the same. It's much more interesting than just sitting in a car.

Think About Who You Want to Take With You—or Who You Can Talk to Before You Go

Before you travel somewhere new, consider taking someone with you who knows the area. If that's not possible, talk to someone who's been there before you go. I've often been that point of contact for people.

One woman, before heading to Kenya, knew I had lived there. She spent a long time talking with me—asking what I recommended, where she should go, and what she should see. It made a huge difference for her trip.

Getting advice from someone who's lived in a place will point you toward the best experiences—and help you avoid the mistakes tourists sometimes make.

When you get there, do the same thing. Talk to local people. Ask them what you should see and do. Locals are almost always the best guides.

Once you've found places you want to visit, try to go with a local if you can. Locals will make sure you see the best of the country—and they'll help you avoid anything dangerous or harmful. They're there to protect you, but they're also there to open doors you might never have found on your own.

It's also a way to build valuable contacts. Sure, you can Google information—but it's much more exciting to hear firsthand stories from people who've lived it.

Then when you arrive, keep asking. Talk to people on the ground. They'll usually steer you toward the most memorable experiences.

Takeaway

To sum up, there are plenty of ways to have fun while traveling that don't center around food and drinking. The best way to discover them is to stay open to new experiences, think ahead about how you want to get where you're going, pay attention to the signs and surroundings once you arrive, focus on what you truly enjoy, and take the time to ask locals for their advice.

Chapter 4

Culture and Religion

Imagine living or working overseas. Instead of seeing new ways of doing things as a challenge, you embrace different cultures and religions as an exciting opportunity—a chance to think about the world in a new way, filled with fresh perspectives.

You might discover the beauty of a culture or religion you never really thought about before. It can be inspiring, wonderful, and eye-opening. Seeing life through another lens can give you insights, new ideas, and possibilities you wouldn't have found otherwise. How you view different religions and cultures adds spice to life and makes it more interesting.

I remember when I first joined the U.S. Peace Corps and was assigned to Gorgora, on the north shore of Lake Tana—the lake that feeds into the Blue Nile River. Everything was different from my home in Los Angeles, but it wasn't frightening.

It was interesting, challenging, and exciting. There was no electricity or running water. I used a Petromax lantern for light and collected water from the lake, purifying it through a large filtration apparatus. We ate different food—and we ate with our hands.

The local religion was Christianity, but it was the Ethiopian Orthodox tradition, which was very different from the Church of Christ I attended in Los Angeles. I loved every minute of it.

The Ethiopian teachers I worked alongside were welcoming and helpful. I even made friends with some British teachers living in Gondar, and they would sometimes visit Gorgora, bringing sandwiches. I swam in the lake regularly and loved it.

That experience in Gorgora made every other unusual living condition I encountered later seem manageable. If I could spend three years there— and thrive—I knew I could live anywhere. The key was always making friends with local people. They knew how to live well in their own culture and circumstances, and they helped make sure I could too, even when everything around me was so different from my familiar life in California.

Our sense of joy often comes from how deeply we engage with our own culture. In the U.S., that might mean going to baseball or football games, concerts, movies, or family gatherings. Living overseas can be just as joyful—but it takes embracing the new cultures and religions around you. And that's exactly what this chapter is about.

Watch Regional Sports and Embrace the Religions

I want your time overseas to be filled with joy, and one of the best ways to experience that joy is by diving into local culture—including sports and religion. Sports are just as central to many cultures as they are in America.

When I lived in Pakistan, for example, cricket was an obsession. You must see the rivalry between the Indian and Pakistani cricket teams to believe it. It's the same in Greece, where soccer reigns supreme. The passion Greeks have for soccer is incredible to witness. Wherever you are, seek out the national sport. Go to a match. Go to a game. It will not only be exciting—it will also open doors to new friendships. You can start by asking coworkers or friends if they'll take you to a game, concert, or event. Or you can simply attend on your own and stay open to meeting new people.

While living in Lahore, Pakistan, I was invited to a wedding where Pakistan's most famous singer and songwriter, Nusrat Fateh Ali Khan, performed. He sang in Urdu. I spoke a few words, but not enough to understand. Thankfully, a man standing nearby volunteered to translate.

The lyrics were passionate and loving—songs about Allah's love for humanity and our love for Allah. When I asked him about it, he said, "This is the loving Islam that you know nothing about." He was right. At the time, like many Americans, I had a limited—and mostly negative—understanding of Islam. That night opened my heart to a very different side of the religion: the beauty of Sufi Islam, full of music, dance, poetry, and love. It led me to read many books and dive deeper into Sufi traditions.

After Pakistan, I was posted to the American Embassy in Khartoum, Sudan. When I arrived, I asked one of the local employees, "Do you have any Sufis here in Khartoum?" He laughed and said, "Oh my God, this place is lousy with Sufis." I asked if he could introduce me to some. He did—and that led to one of the richest experiences of my life. I met many Sufi leaders who welcomed me warmly. They answered all my questions, poured endless cups of tea.

Later, they took me outside to witness traditional Sufi dancing. The Sufi dances—full of whirling and unified, rhythmic movements—trace back to traditions from ancient Persia and Turkey. The goal is to reach a trance-like state where you can connect with the divine. Of course, the dances are accompanied by wonderful drumming.

So, what am I telling you? This is the pattern I've followed again and again living overseas: A meeting, a conversation, or a book opens the door to a new experience, which leads to more exploration, new learning, and new adventures.

Unfortunately, many Americans stay inside their hotel or workplace and miss all of this. But the people at your hotel or workplace can recommend safe, fascinating places to go. Those recommendations can lead to new friends and memories you'll carry with you forever. Curiosity—the willingness to explore and engage—is what makes all the difference.

One of the unexpected gifts from my time exploring Sufi traditions in Sudan was a pair of Sudanese shoes. A friend took me to an elderly shoemaker. The man asked me to stand barefoot on a piece of paper, and he traced the outlines of my feet. From that paper, he crafted a pair of Sudanese shoes: sturdy leather soles with soft leather uppers. They looked like simple slippers— the kind Sudanese people wear everywhere, from sandy roads to city streets.

I bought those shoes in 1995. It's now 2025— and I still wear them every day as house slippers. They have no tears, no holes, no flaws. They are as perfect today as the day he made them.

Don't Forget the Food

In many African and Asian cultures, food is about much more than eating—it's about connection. It's common to sit around a large round pan, sharing handfuls of food with others. Usually, it's rice-based dishes or bread used to scoop the food. Eating with your hands builds friendships.

You talk. You laugh. You discuss food, the day, politics, everything. Many cultures believe that eating with a spoon or fork isn't really eating. Touching the food, sharing it, and passing it to others is part of the experience. It's about more than just nourishment—it's about connection.

Religion and Culture: Twin Pillars of Connection

As much as culture can bring joy into your experience overseas, religion can do the same. Culture is the bedrock of a people's soul. Religion is often its most important expression. To truly engage with people abroad, you have to engage with both their culture and their religion.

The religions I've encountered began with my upbringing in the Church of Christ, a Protestant evangelical church. In Europe, I saw stunning Lutheran and Catholic churches—filled with beautiful paintings, sculptures, and music. Some of Europe's most gorgeous architecture and music can be found inside these churches.

In Muslim countries, I visited majestic mosques in major cities and cozy, intimate neighborhood mosques. Inside, you'll hear practiced voices reciting beautiful prayers.

In India, I visited incredible Hindu temples— each one vibrant with color, tradition, and life. And you can find houses of worship everywhere you go.

Let Go of Assumptions, Live the Language, Learn the Culture

In my early years, after graduating from Pepperdine University, I joined the United

States Peace Corps. I found a tear-off notice in a supermarket in Austin, Texas, and decided to apply. Not long after, I received a one-way ticket to Philadelphia. I called the Peace Corps to thank them—and to ask, "What happens next?" They asked if I had received the packet, and when I said no, they told me, "Three days after you arrive in Philadelphia, you'll fly to Ethiopia to begin your service." It was good to know. At least now I knew how to pack—or thought I did. Truthfully, I still wasn't sure what to bring and knew I needed to travel light.

When I arrived in Addis Ababa, Ethiopia's capital city, we began orientation. The American staff gave us long lists of things to be careful about: food safety, water purification, hygiene. To newly arrived volunteers, it sounded daunting. Then the Ethiopian staff got up and said, "Pay attention to what the American staff told you—but remember, a lot of Ethiopians are still alive." It was their way of reminding us that Ethiopia wasn't as dangerous or overwhelming as we might think. As a result, I learned an important lesson: when you travel, it's important to let go of your assumptions and be open.

After orientation, we traveled south to Dilla in the Sidamo province to learn Amharic, Ethiopia's national language. Most volunteers stayed close to the training center, studying from their books. Tony Zuniga and I took a different approach. We went to the local bars, struck up conversations, and practiced the language by actually using it. We learned the language, not just by studying, but by living the language.

After language training, we were assigned to our posts. Some volunteers became medical workers, while others, like me, became teachers. I took a long, bumpy bus ride from Dilla to Gondar in the north. After checking into a hotel, I set out to find the principal of the school where I was supposed to work. I met Atto Kinde Wassi and explained that I was his new Peace Corps teacher. He was surprised—he hadn't received any official notice. I told him about our language training in Dilla, and once he realized that part was true, he accepted me. When you learn the language and live it, you never know what opportunities can occur.

My school was a junior secondary school in Gorgora, a village about an hour's bus ride from Gondar. Gorgora sits on the northern shore of Lake Tana, Ethiopia's largest lake and the source of the Blue Nile. I found a place to live by sharing a small cottage with another teacher. I quickly got to know the other teachers and my students, and that's when my real cultural education began. We had a cook, and meals were eaten communally from a large round metal pan. Eating with my hands was my first culture lesson—and soon after, I learned another: you must eat with your right hand.

Learn the Rules

One thing I've found in many cultures is that strict adherence to literal truth isn't always followed, expected, or even wanted. It's often better to tell people what they want to hear. Take food, for example. You may not like what you're served, but I'd advise you to praise the wonderful food you've just eaten, whether you liked it or not. That's the polite thing to do, and it keeps relationships friendly. You should also expect that not everything you hear will be strictly true.

People will often tell you what they think you want to hear, and that's part of keeping peace and harmony. If you get to know someone well and build a strong friendship, you might eventually have deeper, more truthful conversations. But be careful what you wish for—you might find that brutal honesty isn't always as satisfying as you imagine.

Another important custom I learned is that in many places, particularly among Orthodox Christians and Muslims, the right hand is considered the clean hand. It's the hand you eat with, shake hands with, and use to hand over objects. The left hand is considered unclean because it's used for personal hygiene. Using your left hand to eat or to hand anything to someone is a deliberate insult and seen as the height of rudeness. I know what you're probably thinking, I thought the same thing. Sometimes I use my right hand in the bathroom too, and my left hand is as clean as my right. But that's not the point. The tradition is what matters. Best to keep your personal habits to yourself and simply respect the customs you're living among. The right hand is clean, and the left hand is unclean, no matter what the reality might be.

There's a broader lesson here, too. You don't need to disclose everything about yourself. It's often better to go along with traditions, even if it means bending the truth a little. You won't always like the truth people might tell you, and they may not like yours. Polite conversation, especially at the beginning of a relationship, often requires avoiding hard truths that could cause offense. Over time, as you build deeper trust, you can explore more frank and honest discussions. But early on, kindness and tact will take you much farther than blunt honesty.

When I joined the U.S. Foreign Service, we adopted an unofficial motto: "Peace through Obfuscation." Obfuscation, after all, means "the act of obscuring something to make it harder to understand." Lawyers are sometimes accused of it, since legal contracts can be almost unreadable. But the truth is, peace often requires something less than the whole, brutal truth. Respect the culture and religion of your hosts in every way you can. They will usually show you the same courtesy. The last thing you want to do is argue about the pros and cons of your culture and theirs. It's always better to say kind, approving words about their traditions without any hint of superiority.

In fact, one of the most interesting things about living abroad is seeing America through other people's eyes. That only happens when you establish genuine, respectful relationships. Otherwise, people will politely hold back their real opinions.

I also learned another important custom: never pass gas in public. Ethiopians tell a story about a woman who was drawing water from a well when the sound of the water in her bucket made a noise like passing gas. She was so ashamed—believing everyone thought she had passed gas—that she killed herself. It might sound extreme to Americans, but it shows how seriously customs are taken.

I don't want this to sound intimidating. Once you know the rules, life becomes easy and even fun. The Ethiopians were incredibly kind and gracious when they taught me their customs because they genuinely wanted me to feel happy and safe in my new home.

During my time there, I attended many weddings, which were full of music, food, and celebration. I visited the village's Ethiopian Orthodox Church and explored the remnants of the Italian occupation—monuments left behind from when the Italians invaded Ethiopia before World War II, only to be driven out by British forces under General Wingate.

Food played a big part in village life. One custom I didn't particularly enjoy was when other people at the table would grab a handful of food and place it directly in my mouth. It was uncomfortable, but out of respect for the culture, I accepted it. I smiled, opened my mouth, and ate.

One of my favorite memories was helping to bring something entirely new to the village. Thanks to a British friend living in Gondar who owned a small gasoline-powered generator and a projector, we were able to show movies. No one in the village had ever seen a movie before. This was a village without piped water or electricity—certainly without theaters. We set up a screen and played short films. In larger cities, every movie began with a clip of Emperor Haile

Selassie. When his image appeared, everyone in the village stood in respect.

Speaking of Haile Selassie, a word or two is deserved. Before becoming Emperor, his childhood name was Lij (meaning "child") Tafari Makonnen. Later, he earned the title Ras Tafari, meaning "Lord Tafari." When he ascended the throne in 1930, he took the name Haile Selassie, which translates to "the Power of the Trinity." His story is legendary. I was told that before becoming emperor, he visited Jamaica, a country then suffering a long drought. When he stepped off the plane, it started raining. Many Jamaicans considered this a divine sign. When he became emperor, Jamaicans who admired him founded the Rastafarian movement—taking their name from Ras Tafari.

Jamaicans later moved to Ethiopia, settling in an area that Haile Selassie himself visited. One day, as I was walking out of a hotel in that region, he walked in with his entourage. We passed each other just three feet apart. His birthday, July 23rd, happened to be the same as mine. When we arrived in Ethiopia, the country was celebrating his 80th birthday. I liked to joke that all those celebrations were actually for me. At one of the events, everyone danced, and I did my best to mimic their moves. Months later, I told some Ethiopian friends about my attempt to dance like them. They laughed and said that the Ethiopians had been trying to mimic my dancing. So you can imagine the mismatched, joyful chaos of that celebration.

There are important lessons in that story. Wherever you go, work hard to adopt the customs of your host country. People around the world often hold Americans and Europeans in great awe and respect. While you might be trying to learn their ways, they may be watching you carefully and trying to copy yours. The exchange of cultures goes both ways.

In Ethiopia, both young and older Peace Corps volunteers noticed something special: respect for elders. In many parts of Africa, Asia, and elsewhere, older people are revered for their wisdom and experience—much more so than in the United States. The older volunteers loved it. And so did I. In every country I've lived in, I've reflected on what I missed about America—and what new gifts I discovered overseas. Respect for elders was one of those gifts.

Takeaways

As I mentioned earlier, religion is a powerful vehicle of culture. Religion shapes everyday life: how people eat, what they value, how they celebrate family, and how they offer hospitality. Some of the world's most breathtaking structures are places of worship. Most of them welcome visitors, though there are sometimes conditions—like removing your shoes, covering your head, or dressing modestly. I recommend visiting as many as you can. The beauty is unforgettable.

Learn what you can about the religions you encounter. It will give you powerful insights into the character and heart of the people. Every culture I've encountered holds hospitality as a sacred duty. Even the poorest families will proudly offer a guest something to eat or drink. It's a matter of pride—and a beautiful, universal gesture of kindness.

Many religions are more similar than they are different. Judaism, Christianity, and Islam, for example, all share common roots. Sadly, it's often those who have the most in common who end up in conflict. Civil wars and religious violence are tragic reminders of how divisions can form even among close cousins. But where violence and hatred exist, so too do kindness, compassion, wisdom, and justice.

The only way to experience a culture fully is to engage with it. Explore. Ask respectful questions. Attend services. Visit places of worship. Eat the food that's offered to you when you can. Learn what makes people in other parts of the world who they are. Most of all, you'll find that everywhere in the world, parents love their children, communities support their elders, and acts of charity and kindness are alive and well.

Be smart, be careful, be curious. Ask questions. Learn. Experience all you can. It will expand your horizons in ways you can't yet imagine— and help you see the beautiful variety and deep similarities among all the peoples of the world.

Chapter 5

Learning or Addressing Ignorance

While visiting Taiwan with my husband, the Taiwanese government took us across the country, and we saw everything. Toward the end of the trip, I met with a gentleman from the Ministry of Foreign Affairs. He asked me how the visit had been and what I thought. I said, "It was really wonderful. Thank you very much." I mentioned that Master Cheng Yen had wanted to meet with me, but I hadn't had the time.

He said, "That's a big mistake."

I said, "Why?"

He said, "Well, it's hard to get a meeting with Master Cheng Yen, and if she wanted to meet you and you didn't, that's a big mistake."

I felt awful.

A year later, I visited South Korea for a UN education conference and made a special trip back to Taiwan to meet with Master Cheng Yen. I finally met her—with my husband. She is Taiwan's Mother Teresa. The Taiwanese would love for her to receive a Nobel Peace Prize, as Mother Teresa did. But because she's Taiwanese, and given the tensions between Taiwan and China, it probably won't happen.

Before I met her, I didn't realize her importance in Taiwan. She's the only female Dharma Master and leads a Buddhist humanitarian organization with operations all over the world, even in mainland China—no small feat considering the political tensions.

She's a powerful woman. I've seen wealthy people visit her and make large donations to fund her incredible work. People deeply respect her and what she stands for. But I had to work to figure out who she was and how she started. I'm so impressed with her. She's in her 80s and has lived with a serious heart condition for most of her life.

She's never left Taiwan, primarily because of her heart. She stays at her home in Hualien, called The Abode. She usually has a medical drip because of her condition, yet she keeps going. Even today, since New York has many Tzu Chi facilities, I stay connected with them. In fact, they've asked me to speak at an interfaith service next week. I always ask how she's doing. They always tell me, "She still has her heart condition, but she's okay." She just keeps going. I always worry that one day I'll hear that she's gone, but thankfully, she continues on.

Be Open to New Cultures and Ways of Living

Master Cheng Yen has a small place where she receives visitors. She sits in a chair, and people come to meet her. When I met her, she said something in Taiwanese. I responded, "I've been to Taiwan before, but I haven't been to Hualien before."

People in the audience gasped, saying, "Oh my God, you understand Taiwanese!"

I said, "Well, no, not really. I just assumed she was asking if I had been to Taiwan before—that's what people usually ask."

I didn't actually understand the words, but I understood the meaning.

People thought I was special because of that and said, "You must have an affinity with Master Cheng Yen."

I said, "Okay, I'll take that."

She and her entire organization were so gracious. We drank many cups of tea, ate lots of rice, and they invited my husband and me to stay the night at The Abode.

We attended morning services at 5 a.m.—not my favorite time to be awake. A lot of it involved kneeling, which I'm not very good at, so it was uncomfortable. But I wanted to follow the customs, so I did my best. When they bowed, I bowed. When they knelt, I knelt. They even gave me pillows because they could tell my knees were hurting. A lot of the elderly people there had the same issues. There were chimes and drums, and a sense of solemnity, though it was very different from the religions I was used to. It was interesting, and because I stayed open to the experience, I got so much out of it.

Master Cheng Yen invited Isaac and me to join her for a meal—all vegetarian, of course. Buddhists don't eat meat. The food was wonderful. I said, "I could be a vegetarian forever if I had this kind of food!"

When you travel, stay curious. Adapt where you can, and that openness will always pay off.

How to Be Curious and Humble When You're in a New Country

One of the best ways to address ignorance and focus on learning is by staying curious and humble when you're visiting another country. Make sure you're talking to important people. Remember, every person you meet has a culture, a religion, a family, a background.

The more you can learn about their heritage, beliefs, and values—the things that really matter to them—the stronger the rapport you'll build.

And expect the same from them.

People will often ask, "Where are you from?"

"What's your background?"

"Who are your people?"

"What do you believe?"

The more you have those conversations, the more you build mutual respect.

You'll also learn more about the culture itself, which may be very different from what you're used to. Even though New York City has nearly every culture represented—including Buddhist organizations like Tzu Chi—it's different experiencing it in its original setting.

When I was posted in Greece for my first Foreign Service assignment, someone asked me, "Do you know what the second-largest Greek city is in the world?"

I asked, "What?"

They answered, "New York City."

That stuck with me. You can find the whole world in New York—but nothing replaces experiencing a place firsthand.

Also, anything you can learn ahead of time—through books, articles, or even a quick Google search—will help. Now, you can Google Taiwan, Buddhism in Taiwan, or Master Cheng Yen and learn so much before even getting on a plane. The more you prepare, the better your experience will be.

Questions to ask to learn more about people and the country you're visiting

Before you ask anyone questions, think about:

- What are you curious about?
- What are you hoping to understand?
- What matters most to you?

When you focus your curiosity, you'll ask better, deeper questions—and you'll come away with a richer experience.

Takeaway

If you're ever given the opportunity to meet someone important, take it. I was lucky enough to get a second chance to meet Master Cheng Yen, and it changed me.

When you're in a new country, seek out meaningful conversations. Be curious, be humble, and treat the people you meet the way you'd want to be treated. Learn about the country ahead of time, and when you're there, don't be afraid to ask questions—but always ask with respect, openness, and genuine curiosity.

Chapter 6

Be Careful Out There

I've never been robbed or hurt overseas. With some luck and precautions, you can be safe too. Living and working overseas has been a wonderful and fulfilling experience for me.

When you live abroad, you'll see how much other nations learn from the United States—they often adopt many of our laws, democratic processes, and business practices. And we can return the favor by learning from them. We all get better when we exchange experiences and ideas.

Take Care of Your Physical Safety

When it comes to physical safety, we need all the learning we can muster.

My husband and I live in New York City. We have a smoke alarm in our one-bedroom apartment.

Our building has a front desk where visitors are checked in—staff will call us to ask if we want someone allowed up. Fire departments, police, and emergency medical help are available if needed. Fortunately, we haven't had to use these services ourselves, but neighbors have.

When you live and work overseas, you need to think about safety just as seriously. All the services we count on in New York are just as necessary abroad. During many of my U.S. diplomatic assignments overseas, we had armed guards at our gates. It's critical to know how to contact emergency services: fire department, police, and medical help.

We're also cautious walking around New York. We stay alert to our surroundings and avoid dark or isolated streets at night. Taking these same precautions overseas has kept us safe in many locations.

You need to know what to expect wherever you go.

For example, children in Rome are notorious pickpockets. I visited Rome with an Indian friend. He wasn't protecting his belongings, and I knew he would lose something if I didn't intervene. I had him give me his passport, money, and credit cards. I tucked both our valuables close to my body under layers of clothing. Despite my warnings, a group of children tried to pick my pockets—but I stayed far away and moved quickly to safe spots.

They managed to reach into my friend's pockets and grabbed whatever they found. They ran to a tree, opened their haul, and found nothing but lint and scrap paper. They actually brought it all back to him. When we got back to the hotel, I handed him back his real valuables.

Bring Your Street Smarts with You

Being prepared for the worst can make a big difference.

At the U.S. Embassy in Athens, I met many Americans who had lost their valuables to pickpockets and scammers. When I asked them if they had talked to strangers or wandered down dark streets, the answer was usually yes. I'd ask where they were from—Detroit, Dallas, Los Angeles, and so on. I'd follow up: "Would you do that in your hometown?" And inevitably, they'd say no—they'd be more careful at home.

The truth is: every precaution you take at home is just as necessary—and maybe even more so—overseas.

Another important tip: don't wear flashy jewelry. A friend of mine wore a pretty gold necklace while walking with her boyfriend one night in Nairobi. A group of boys tore the necklace right off her neck. Her boyfriend's first instinct was to chase after them—but he made the smarter decision to stay and protect her.

Stuff is replaceable. People are not.

If you must wear jewelry for a gala or event, keep it hidden until you're inside. Put it back out of sight before leaving.

In short: whatever precautions you take in Detroit, Dallas, or New York, double them when you're overseas.

Health

When traveling or living overseas, be prepared for the local health conditions. Visit your doctor or a travel clinic before you go. Get any necessary vaccinations for your destination. If you'll be in an area where malaria is a risk, you'll need anti-malaria medication—and daily doses at that.

You should also do all you can to avoid mosquito bites, which are how malaria spreads:

- Use insecticides in your home.
- Install mesh screens on windows and doors.
- Sleep under a mosquito net at night.

Consult health professionals to make sure you have the right medications, vaccines, and safety gear for where you're headed.

Also, when walking outside, wear boots and socks—especially if you're unsure about the safety of the area. Avoid walking barefoot in unfamiliar places where bacteria or parasites could be a risk.

I know all this sounds a little scary. It's supposed to—because taking precautions matters. But once you get used to dressing for safety, taking your medications, and preparing your home, it becomes second nature. What feels unusual at first soon becomes routine.

And honestly, many areas of the world don't require any special precautions at all. Do your research. Consult experts. Living and working overseas can be a joy and an amazing adventure. Staying healthy and safe just helps you enjoy it more.

If you'll be abroad for a while, research the nearest healthcare facility ahead of time. I've had major surgeries in Nairobi, Kenya and Johannesburg, South Africa—with excellent results. I've consulted doctors in London. Healthcare worldwide is often excellent—and sometimes much more affordable than in the U.S. Many people even travel to India for surgery because the quality of care is high and costs are lower.

Stay Vigilant, Not Fearful

This book isn't here to scare you. It's here to prepare you. Bad things can happen anywhere—even in developed countries. Canadian friends of ours had $3,000 stolen from a hotel safe in New York City—with the hotel taking no responsibility. Visitors have caught tick-borne West Nile virus right here too. No place is immune.

Stay vigilant everywhere: whether you're in Africa, Asia, Latin America, or Western cities.

The goal isn't to live in fear. The goal is to enjoy the world's wonders while keeping yourself safe.

Talk to people you trust. Hotel staff and work colleagues are often happy to tell you which places are great to visit—and which places to avoid.

A good rule of thumb: whatever you do to protect yourself at home, do even more of it abroad.

Learn from Others

Before I visited Vietnam for the first time, I spoke to someone who had been there many times. I learned a lot from him, and both my trips to Vietnam were wonderful. The traffic was chaotic—but I got used to it. The Vietnamese people were kind and gracious.

I kept apologizing for the Vietnam War. They gently corrected me: "In Vietnam, we call it the American War." And they didn't seem to carry a grudge. They treated my husband and me with respect and kindness.

That said, I recommend visiting the War Remembrance Museum in Ho Chi Minh City (formerly Saigon). The museum documents the effects of Agent Orange and the war's devastation. It's hard to see, but important. The museum shows how much Ho Chi Minh admired the U.S. Constitution—and how hard he tried to win American support against French colonialism. Sadly, both Europe and America only supported self-determination for European nations—not for African or Asian ones.

One of the biggest gifts of living abroad is experiencing how others see America.

American media doesn't always give us that view. You'll find that, around the world, there's deep admiration for America—our power, democracy, and standard of living. But there's also bewilderment: how could a great nation so often betray its own values?

Seeing America through other people's eyes changes you. It's humbling. It's necessary.

Stay Aware of Current Events

Events can happen—or stop happening— very quickly. Many countries participate in demonstrations, especially places like France and Kenya. In both countries, people take to the streets quickly to protest government actions or international concerns.

Once, when I was in France with my husband, we had a wonderful trip. When we were ready to leave, we booked a train to London. But massive demonstrations broke out, and the trains stopped running. We couldn't get to London that day. We simply walked across the street from the train station, found a very nice little hotel, and spent the night. The next day, the demonstrations ended, and we caught our train.

In many countries, it's not unusual for planes, trains, and other services to stop temporarily due to protests. Usually, things are back to normal within a day or two. You can almost always find a hotel or a safe place to wait it out.

I also had a friend preparing to travel to Kenya. We had a long conversation before she left. Just before her trip, I saw news reports about large demonstrations over a new tax law that people were protesting. I warned her that she might want to postpone her trip. She decided to go anyway. By the time she arrived, the demonstrations had ended, and she had a wonderful time in Kenya.

Remember, demonstrations happen in the United States too—and around the world. While they can certainly be inconvenient for travelers, frankly, I often find myself supporting the demonstrators. The protests in Kenya worked—the new tax law was repealed.

Here in the United Staes, women have demonstrated for reproductive rights, and people around the world have protested for different causes. I'm a liberal, and I usually support peaceful demonstrations.

That said, it's important to acknowledge that not all demonstrations stay peaceful. We saw that clearly on January 6th at the U.S. Capitol, where violence led to the deaths of Capitol police officers.

Sadly, these kinds of violent demonstrations can—and do—happen in other countries as well. My advice: stay out of the way. If demonstrations break out, find a nice hotel or restaurant, relax, and wait for the calm to return.

Takeaway

To sum up, there are three keys to staying safe abroad:

- Take care of your physical safety.
- Take care of your health.
- Learn from others—both before you go and while you're there.

Do these things, and you'll not only stay safe—
you'll get to experience everything the world has
to offer.

Photos from Bruce's Travels

In my efforts to enact same-sex marriage in Taiwan, I met with the Vice President who is Catholic. I believe I persuaded him to not oppose same sex marriage which was eventually enacted in Taiwan.

Another photo at the same meeting with the VP of Taiwan.

I spoke at Tschinwa University in Beijing China. It is the most important university in China. Chinese President Xi Jinping graduated from Tschinwa University. The students were receptive to my remarks about LGBT rights, but no progress has been made in China. Many Chinese students in the USA are more open about their sexual orientation than they are in China.

Speaking in favor of LGBT rights at the UN General Assembly in NYC. My husband, Isaac took this photo.

My husband Isaac Humphrie and I went to a Unitarian Church in Brooklyn. Bernie Sanders arrived and spoke as he was campaigning for the democratic party's nomination for President. We got a photo op with him in the back room of the church.

I was invited to an LGBT meeting at the Obama White House and this photo was taken of me by a White House photographer. After this meeting, we went to the residence of Vice President Joe Biden for dinner.

Speaking together with Chinese diplomat Dr. Guo at the United Nations.

This is the Abode, the home of the Dharma Master of the Buddhist Tzu Chi Foundation, which is a global foundation, much like Mother Teresa's Sisters of Charity. The Dharma Master, Chen Yen has a heart condition and she is in her 80's as was Mother Teresa when I met her. Master Chen Yen asked me not to say that she was either for or against same-sex marriage in Taiwan. I said that I would, of course abide by her wishes, but I asked, "Can I say that you and your entire Foundation have been gracious and kind to me and my husband." She said, yes, I could say that. I told everyone in met in Taiwan that the very famous Dharma Master Chen Yen was gracious and kind to me and my husband and that actions speak louder than words, so they could decide for themselves if Master Chen Yen endorsed same-sex marriage or not.

I was lobbying for same-sex marriage in Taiwan. Every year since 2017, I've been invited to speak to the World League of Freedom and Democracy in Taipei. This used to be called the Anti-Communist League. After of our meetings at the Grand hotel we met Taiwanese government officials. I was there with my husband and we met the Foreign Minister, and one of his staff took this photo.

This photo needs some commentary. I was posted to the U.S. Consulate General at Lahore Pakistan. First Lady, Hilary Clinton was on her way by plane from the USA to Lahore. I got a call from the U.S. Embassy in Islamabad. They told me that there was a threat on Hilary's life. I asked what I should do. I was told, "Stay Alert." I did. Hilary spoke at the University of Lahore and then had a lavish reception at the Lahore fort hosted by the Pakistani Prime Minister, Benazir Bhutto. Then Hilary and Benazir came back to the Lahore airport where I was in the VIP lounge with other Americans. When they arrived, Hilary asked Benazir to have a seat, because Hilary wanted to meet the Americans. I was the first

American she met. We had a brief conversation. White House photographers took our photos. I threw them all away because they all showed the back of my head- and full-on Hilary's face. A Pakistani photographer friend of mine took the photo below and he framed it and gave it to me. His photo was much more attractive than the White House photos. Later, when Hilary was running for President, I met her again in Washington D.C. and reminded her that we'd met in Pakistan. She said that as President she would pay particular attention to Pakistan.

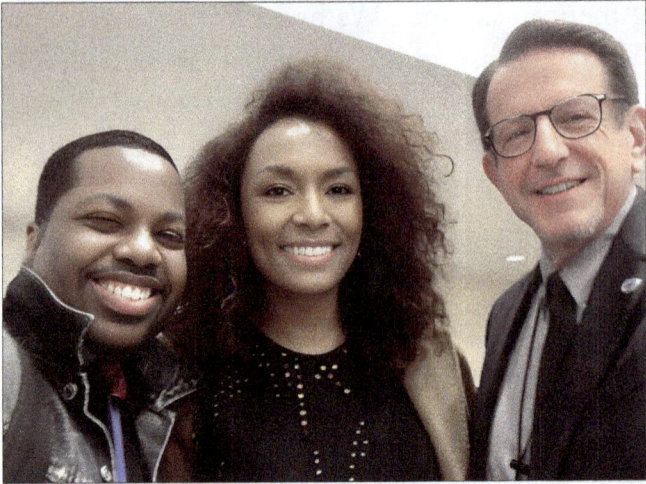

I was able to mainstream LGBT rights at the United Nations. In my decades of work on LGBT rights, I've always said that the T standing for Trans people are the most endangered. I worked very hard to highlight Trans rights. Janet Mock is a prominent Trans activist and I organized getting her to speak at the UN. Later my husband and I took a photo with her.

I met with a Lesbian Attorney in Seoul Korea.
We worked together to support LGBT rights in
South Korea. I was not as successful in Korea as
I was in Taiwan.

I was speaking at the World League of Freedom and Democracy, in Taiwan, and President Ma, who was the nation's president at the time was also a featured speaker. Later we when to his office and afterwards we got photo ops with President Ma.

www.ingramcontent.com/pod-product-compliance
Lightning Source LLC
Chambersburg PA
CBHW070133100426
42744CB00009B/1817